Best of
Banana Slicer
Reviews
(Part Uno)

Señor Mateo Lütz
El Valiente

ISBN: 153481423X
ISBN-13: 978-1534814233

DEDICATION

I dedicate this book to the previous 570 versions of the Hutzler 571 Banana Slicer. Without you, none of this would be possible ... or necessary.

CONTENTS

ACKNOWLEDGMENTS

This book is made possible only through the comedic genius of the many reviewers of this legendary Banana Slicer. Without them, this book would not be possible, and the world would be filled with far fewer giggles.

Also, tip o' the cap to the engineers and thought leaders behind the wonder that is the Hutzlet 571 Banana Slicer. Without their creative prowess, unwavering fortitude, and sheer stick-to-itiveness through the previous 570 failed versions, the future of this planet, and the species who inhabit it, would be questionable, at best.

THE REVIEWS ARE IN!

No more winning for you, Mr. Banana!

For decades I have been trying to come up with an ideal way to slice a banana. "Use a knife!" they say. Well...my parole officer won't allow me to be around knives. "Shoot it with a gun!" Background check...HELLO! I had to resort to carefully attempt to slice those bananas with my bare hands. 99.9% of the time, I would get so frustrated that I just ended up squishing the fruit in my hands and throwing it against the wall in anger. Then, after a fit of banana-induced rage, my parole officer introduced me to this kitchen marvel and my life was changed. No longer consumed by seething anger and animosity towards thick-skinned yellow fruit, I was able to concentrate on my love of theatre and am writing a musical play about two lovers from rival gangs that just try to make it in the world. I think I'll call it South Side Story. Banana slicer...thanks to you, I see greatness on the horizon.

Saved my marriage

What can I say about the 571B Banana Slicer that hasn't already been said about the wheel, penicillin, or the iPhone.... this is one of the greatest inventions of all time. My husband and I would argue constantly over who had to cut the day's banana slices. It's one of those chores NO ONE wants to do! You know, the old "I spent the entire day rearing OUR children, maybe YOU can pitch in a little and cut these bananas?" and of course, "You think I have the energy to slave over your damn bananas? I worked a 12 hour shift just to come home to THIS?!" These are the things that can destroy an entire relationship. It got to the point where our children could sense the tension. The minute I heard our 6-year-old girl in her bedroom, re-enacting our daily banana fight with her Barbie dolls, I knew we had to make a change. That's when I found the 571B Banana Slicer. Our marriage has never been healthier, AND we've even incorporated it into our lovemaking!

Angle is wrong

I tried the banana slicer and found it unacceptable. As shown in the picture, the slicer is curved from left to right. All of my bananas are bent the other way.

NOT wifi capable???

Maybe I'm doing it wrong, but I can't get this thing hooked up to my wifi network. Am I supposed to slice my bananas over an ethernet cable? What is this, 2005?

Kirk Cameron's banana slicer

If God does not exist, then how is it that a banana fits so perfectly in this banana slicer?
CHECKMATE, ATHEISTS!

Just okay

It's kind of cheaply made, but it works better than the hammer I've been using to slice my bananas.

Confusing

There is no way to tell if this is a standard or metric banana slicer. Additional markings on it would help greatly.

what a lifesaver!!!

i had bananas sitting there going bad cause i had nooo idea how to cut them

WARNING: Does not work on tomatoes!

Does not work on tomatoes. The manufacturer decided to make these yellow therefore making it impossible to use on other fruits!! I hope there will be a new version soon.

Dogs love it!

My dogs recently complained that my bite-sized pieces were uneven and that one would always get slightly more banana than the other. They also appreciate that my spit and mouth bacteria aren't on their precious banana pieces!

Fine if you want boring banana slices

I was really hoping this would put ridges in my banana slices and make them all fancy looking, but, alas, it only produces plain, flat cuts like all the others. How am I supposed to impress my gay friends when they come over for brunch and my fruit slices looks so plain? I'll just have to resort to using my melon baller next time.

Much better than the previous Hutzler Model 570

Much better than the previous Hutzler Model 570, which was a paring knife. Who has time for ancient, proven, useful technology when we can fill our kitchen drawers with gimmicky Chinese junk?

One Star

Irresponsible product. In the hands of the wrong people this technology could threaten civilization.

Life is complete.

We don't use it at all because it's completely nonsensical. But, just HAVING it, knowing we might ONE DAY use it for a smoothie or something (but bananas break apart pretty easily without being sliced so probably not) brings a sense of calm and comfort to the soul.

Great for Dog Turds Too!

Provided it's not old and hardened, this little gadget will slice up a fresh dog turd beautifully. Works equally well for both small and large breeds. Our entire family loves it and we even managed to get the kids to put down their iPhones and join us in the yard!

No training video. No go.

Doesn't come with a manual and training video. USELESS.

Two Stars

Do not, I repeat DO NOT use this on your penis. Ouch!

One Star

Bankrupted my regular butter knife family business of 120 years..screw you hutzler 571

Hoping they come out with left curved cutter ...

works perfectly for all my right curved bananas. highly recommend, hoping they come out with left curved cutter next!

Inferior display technology

The built-in Super AMOLED display only shows yellow?! How am I supposed to get status updates about my slicing on my new Apple Watch?

It ruined my life!

Before this product I was never able to eat bananas. After this product my life was changed... For the worse. The Hutzler 571 got me addicted to bananas. I lost my job, my friends, my family, my dog, and my home due to my obsessive banana consumption. I am currently seeing a support group for people with my exact same problem, but after every meeting we just get together and slice up more bananas. I can't go more than 10 minutes without eating a banana.

Peace, Hope, Love.

Move over sliced bread! Who needs you when we can bulk up on potassium!? The Hutzler 571 Banana Slicer gives hope to a seemingly hopeless world. Dreams really do come true when long bananas can be separated into up to 17 separate sections! I daresay that if this product would have been invented sooner; the titanic would not have sunk, the cold war would have been lukewarm, and Cain probably wouldn't have killed Abel. If such a marvel like this can be invented by mere man, I have faith in the future to come. What more can be built that has had the way paved by such a phenomenon!? As a wise man once said, "Bad analogies are like a banana in a sword fight" well I suspect that no such sword fight would have taken place over a well made banana split. This artifact wakes me up in the morning, stops children from crying, and shines like the yellow sun in the shape of a crescent moon. Buy it. Love it. Live.

The Perfect Gift

Bought this as a birthday gift for my pet chimp Bubbles. Now he uses a toothpick to eat his bananas off a plate - like a dignified chimp.

the best invention since sliced bread

the hutzler 571 is a marvelous product, it rivals german engineering! the best invention since sliced bread! its great for other uses too, like slicing things shaped like bananas, like green bananas and plantains. My favorite feature about this product though is its compatibility with the average american banana, it is perfect size and.... and..... idk all i can say is just buy this product it will change your life, i now can bench 225 and make 500k a year

It's bigger than it looks in the picture.

That's what she said.

This right here is 'Murica

This right here is 'Murica - distilled into a flexible banana shaped shell. If you want metric why don't you go get yourself a plantain slicer? Here in 'Murica we adopt your fruit...make it a staple of our breakfasts, and then redistribute it to the world as if it was our own idea! 'Murica, fuck yeah.

Five Stars

Much improved version over the Hutzler 570 - and it can be used by someone with only 9 fingers!

One Star

My banana's too big for this.

One Star

Unit is now bricked and unusable after failed firmware update to make it compatible with cucumbers

Great idea with one major flaw

It is aimed at lazy people like me, but it just weighs far too much.

This product is getting my life back together

I have struggled for years to eat a banana in public without attracting unwanted attention from men offering sexual favors. Day after day, they would hound me to accompany them into the public restrooms. You can only say no so many times...until you say yes. But now, I can eat these bananas in a tasteful, non-phallic shape. It even works as a book mark for my bible. With this, I am one step away from my wife letting me see the kids again. Thanks Hutzler!

PS – is there a Hutzler website that is mobile friendly? Loading the desktop web page on my phone isn't working because I cant get any signal in these public restrooms.

Actually for bananas?

And here I thought this was a decoy and not for "actual bananas". Will wonders never cease?

Thank god!

Previously I absolutely could not banana. Now... I CAN banana.

Tried eating a banana WITHOUT slicing it and almost paid for it with my life.

Each inconsistent bite went down with the grace of a truck stop hooker. While enjoyable, my throat still screamed, "I just want to be held." I got this banana slicer to change the way I ate bananas, but it did more than that, it changed the way I consumed food.

I started to feel pretty guilty. I mean the screaming. But that's all changed

Very humane banana killer. Their death is painless and quick. No more of those tear-filled, sad banana eyes staring at me while I do what needs to be done in order to have a balanced breakfast.

Update for new version

Still trying to figure out how to update to 572 through iTunes.

Help!

The instructions weren't clear enough. wound up in the ceiling fan.

One Star

It only works if you have a banana, which apparently are not included... such bullshit.

Happy wife is a happy life

When I asked my wife what she wanted for Christmas, she said, "It's 10 inches long, plastic and shaped like a banana." Boom, Christmas handled. Next!

NOT "great for cereal!!"

I tried slicing Cheerios, Trix, Corn Flakes, and Chex, and each ended up smashed, not neatly sliced. What's worse, this thing is completely useless on Cream of Wheat.

Slice a banana but no one else

This is so convenient since my family hid all the knives from me. You stab one person and suddenly you can't slice your own bananas anymore.

No reverse on this thing?

Great for the rich and lazy like myself, but there is no reverse on this thing, so once you begin the slicing, you are committed to the results produced. It takes about 20 minutes of pep time and talking myself into proper line up.

Saved our marriage

My husband was always asking for it so finally..... I got it!!! This product saved our marriage. We're going for a leisurely stroll at the butterfly sanctuary today.

IT'S TOO YELLOW

Love this product, however, I'm refrained of using it on the field because it is too bright. Enemy snipers can detect it from far away and almost got hit at least twice while trying to prepare a mid-combat snack; are you thinking about launching a camouflage series? I'd love to see this product in woodland, 3-color desert or UCP. These would match the Tactical Banana cases I already own.

Five Stars

It'll slice ur banana real good-like.

Hassle-free!

Can't think of any other easy and practical way of slicing bananas. Using a knife, an axe, or a chainsaw is just too taxing.

International Bananas/EU bananas

OK with international bananas but didn't work with my EU imposed straight bananas.... be aware!

Three Stars

Am I supposed to peel the banana first? I'm so confused.

Set your family up for life with this product!!

With recent reports of the Cavendish banana about to go extinct this is certain to become a very hot collectors item in the very near future! Imagine, no bananas will survive but your own sturdy plastic Hutzler 571 Banana Slicer will . You will be one of the lucky few to have this antique item which will symbolize what life with bananas was once like. Never mind saving up for your children's college education, just save a few of these in its original packaging and one trip to Pawn Stars will have your children and grandchildren set for life!! I am thinking of depleting my entire retirement savings to buy every last one of these before production stops, so hurry!!

Stopped working after the OTA update

This piece of junk has stopped working for me after 3 months. One day I found that this had moved from our beloved curio cabinet to a box in the garage labeled "useless crap" I thought that was odd but thought nothing of it, that is until I tried to use it. I only have Dole Bananas on hand if found out after this update the Hutzler 571 gets stuck and hangs about halfway through the process. I tried later with a Chiquita and it works. DO NOT BUY THIS! Good old Hutzler took Sony's lead and made this thing proprietary, in the high stakes multi-million dollar world of fruit cutlery it's obvious no one is looking out for the little guy that just wants some nanners in his Oat Bran

Once every thousand years an advancement in the human condition becomes reality.

As the days feel as dark as night and there appears to be no end to the torment we know as life such as an ex-wife. A shining light appears. One that is so special that it brings a bright flame to a new romance and is even good enough to bring a 9 foot Christmas tree to life in a Jewish home as a cleverly crafted ornament created by a woman's love for her man. At that point it all makes sense, life that is. The universe is the Hutzler 571 banana slicer.

The Hutzler Banana Slicer makes the perfect size banana chunks for the better-than-sex banana pudding cake ...
Nothing else compares.. They say once you go Hutzler, you never go back, and it's true.

No longer must I measure twice before cutting once
Hell, I no longer need to measure at all. Bananas morning, noon, and night. I bathe in bananas with my new banana slicer.

I'd love to use it but...
I just can't bring myself to until I have the entire setup in the second picture. Can someone link me to that bowl and spoon so I can finally eat this banana???

I bought this for my Muslim neighbor for Christmas. ...
well because they don't celebrate Christmas and I felt really sorry for them. They said thank you and tears began running down their faces. They suddenly left the room and returned with 17 ak47's and 12 pipe bombs which they handed over to me. They declared that Jihad is no longer necessary and they wish to live in peace now. I think we should buy these

Hutzler 571 Banana Slicers and send them to Syria and Iraq and just watch the peace break out.

The dawn of an era

We have truly reached the age of enlightenment. As a sociologist I am often asked what innovation I predict as defining the 21st century, smart-phones, social media, the Kardashians? I can now say with total conviction that our century will be known by posterity as the dawn of the Hutzler 571 Banana slicer.

I wasn't thinking when I went through airport security with this in my carry on.

TSA strip searched me, called out bomb sniffing dogs and performed a complete cavity search as I was standing in line. I missed my flight and they placed me on the "No Fly" list. Apparently these are a lot more dangerous than one may think. It's only a matter of time before someone hijacks an airplane with a Hutzler 571.

Additional tool necessary

All these comments about left-handed slicers are stupid. The slicer only goes one direction. All you need is a pair of plastic tongs. They're not even a dollar ($0.92) but there is $7.17 shipping. These are items that should be in the "purchased together" list, Amazon! Use them to flip the banana, people.. Sheesh!

I suffer from a terrible case of lockjaw

… which ironically was caused by trying to take a bite of 10 of my favorite fruit at the same time... Bananas. I was rushed to the hospital after my jaw unhinged and broke from the excessive outward force exerted by the bananas, and my jaw was wired shut. Tragically the average girth of a banana is 1 inch, and due to a genetic bone/ligament deformity the new position of my jaw would not allow my mouth to open more than .5 inches for the rest of my life. I became sad and depressed. Bananas brought me more happiness than even my wife, who instead of asking how I was when she arrived at the hospital, she proceeded to ask "why the f*** were you trying to shove ten bananas down your throat?" I wrote that she wouldn't understand. Nobody understands. Except the Hutzler 571 Banana Slicer, which unfortunately I learned about too late. Learn from me.

WARNING!: Do not use for circumcision.
Is further explanation necessary?

Waiting for lengthwise banana slicer
Imagine our disappointment when we received the banana slicer. We only serve breakfast in long Banana Boat bowls and therefore we find slicing bananas along latitudinal lines is not our style. We will wait for the longitudinal banana slicer to cut bananas vertically downward

Nu-uhhh, it's bad for cereal
It said great with cereal but my fruit loops went straight through. Beware the Hutzler 571

After having delivered a healthy child on a crowded subway ...
...with nothing more than the Hutzler 571 Banana Slicer, I have to give this product 5 out of 5. I require a replacement as the original stayed with the mother.

Thanks to this amazing product, I can now enjoy just the tip ...

... of the banana with no regrets. Thank you 571 Banana Slicer!

Beautiful ornaments for the discerning Christmas tree

LOVE this Christmas ornament! I bought 15 of them for my coworkers as Christmas gifts - we love to exchange ornaments every year and build memories together.

Three Stars

My banana is too long. I need the 571-XL.

No need to stare at the ground anymore!

Woo hoo! Perfect for work. Finally I can make eye contact with people!

No batteries required?

I was hoping it was battery operated-too much effort trying to slice on my own.

Buggy!

Maybe it's the rotten bananas that I'm using, not certain but there seem to be bugs. I downloaded the patch that someone recommended which was a link to a coupon for Raid Ant Spray, that surprisingly was actually helpful.

All Hail the Mighty Hutzler

My family always goes around the Thanksgiving table and says what they are thankful for. Good health, sure; loving family, okay; world peace, whatevs. But this year our centerpiece was a bunch of bananas and everyone could use the Hutzler 571 Banana Slicer. We all cried as everyone took their turn slicing through the banana, it was like slicing a big yellow banana shaped slab of buddha. It was the most beautiful thing we have ever seen.

Bellyful

My boyfriend won't let me use a ruler, so I used this instead. Good to know exactly how much banana is going down my throat.

A Must Have!

This is much faster than my guillotine, easier to clean than my table saw and much quieter and cleaner than running my chainsaw in the kitchen. I don't how I've lived without this!

Color is all wrong

I'm sick and tired of losing my banana slices, they seem to go through the slots then disappear from view. If they would make the slicer a different color than yellow, I could eat my damn slices instead of slipping on them, or worse finding them on my clothes an hour after arriving at work.

Totally useless, needs better documentation

Does this even come with instructions? I can't even figure out how to plug it in. Totally useless, needs better documentation.

Four Stars

Just like me to go and order the Model 570 just before they released this beauty with all the upgrades. Damnit!

Probably the worst invention ever bestowed upon mankind

Probably the worst invention ever bestowed upon mankind, maybe second only to the gas chambers at Auschwitz. Bananas come in different sizes, so to have one generic banana shape makes absolutely no sense. Rot in hell! That is all.

WTF?!?!?

There's got to be an app for this by now! What is this, 2007?!?!?

Failed my kids

While it does cut bananas, the ad says that kids will enjoy slicing their own bananas too. I bought this so that my kids would have something else to do, other than play video games. I even invested in a couple bunches of bananas to encourage their new hobby (a waste of money, as we don't eat fruit). To my disappointment, they couldn't have cared less. When I inquired about other kids at school who have taken up "nanner slicin'" (probably what the kids are calling it), my sons just laughed at me and replied that slicing bananas is "lame". I specifically purchased this as a means to provide my kids with an extracurricular activity, and maybe turn their grades around and get them off of pot. For failing my children I give it 3 stars!

At first we didn't like it cause ...

... some of our bananas were curved the wrong way. Then my brilliant spouse figured out we could do those bananas against the ceiling! We highly recommend this product!

Great addition to any junk drawer!

I knew my kitchen junk drawer was missing something. It has the usual obscure utensils-ice pick, meat hook, those little corn cob sticker things-but it opened so freely. I knew this was unacceptable for any kitchen junk drawer. I needed that one big thing that would barely fit in and would snag the counter every time I opened it. The Hutzler 571 was perfect! Now my drawer snags like every other junk drawer I've ever had and I have to push the Hutzler 571 down with my hand to get it open.

This product made me fat!

While this product is making banana slicing simpler, it is now too simple. I have gained 20 pounds in unburned calories from using the 571B slicer compared to an ordinary knife, which defeats the purpose of eating the yellow fruit in the first place. Would not recommend. BUYER BEWARE

It work for turds also.

But don't put slice turd on cereal, though.

Five Stars

They've done studies, you know. 60% of the time it works every time.

Just don't go in the water with it!

Uh...You're going to need a bigger banana.

Disappointed...

In the description for the Hutzler 571 Banana Slicer, it says "Great for cereal". But I found that it's not great for cereal at all! Not only did it cut my tongue, but it was hard to chew and didn't taste very good. What were they thinking? I'm going back to oatmeal.

No backwards compatibility :(

Bought this for $99 before they dropped the price (I KNOW, early adopter syndrome ugh): Just a heads up, there is NO backwards compatibility between the H-571 or earlier models. So bananas that you sliced with previous models will not work on this one and vice versa. :(

A dream for scouring dead skin and callouses off of your feet

Works like a dream for scouring the dead skin and callouses off of your feet. Self cleaning too... A couple of taps on the trash can and most of the foot scrapings come right off. Back in the drawer ready for slicing bananas.

This product and its subsequent fanfare is...

… genuinely why I love humanity.

This LITERALLY saved my life.

I used to love eating bananas by just shoving the whole thing down into my throat. Then Gwen Stefani came out with that song and I felt all guilty like god was judging me or something. So I stopped eating delicious bananas all together. But how was I to eat all my peanut butter without bananas? Enter the Hutzler 571 Banana Slicer. This baby changed my life! Here I was, on the brink of starvation, surrounded by overripe bananas and uneaten peanut butter with NO way to consume them without being dammed to hell! All of the sudden I'm able to SLICE the bananas and make these little peanut butter banana sandwiches using banana slices as the bread. This thing literally saved my life.

Enhancement request

Gave this 4 stars due to lack of a catching plate underneath which could have been useful when my neighbors wife attacked him In the "sub tropical" area with the banana peeler... Surgery was complicated due to segments 3 and 5 going missing during the fracas, so reconstruction was tricky to say the least but the surgeon assured him that the replacement rubber bushings would hold up for a long time. Recovery is slow but he said he'll bounce back...

Every parent must read

I have used the Hutzler 571 Banana Slicer for several years at home with great success. With the implementation of Common Core Standards it only seemed logical that teaching the youth of our nation the benefits of Hutzler 571 Banana Slicer should be added to the Common Core Curriculum. Upon petitioning the Common Core advisory council for inclusion of the Hutzler 571 Banana Slicer into the standards, it was brought to my attention that a banana has no core and therefore does not meet the stringent requirements set forth for all American Youth. What's next? Eliminating cursive writing instruction? Not saying the Pledge of Allegiance each morning? Eliminating chalkboards? Keep America strong parents and purchase a Hutzler 571 Banana Slicer for home instruction. You are the most important influence in their life. Go give your kid a hug and slice a banana together.

One day, you will see the 571 in the Smithsonian.

Not enough good things can be said about the Hutzler 571. It is a device that this generation desperately needs.

That is annoying..

They fail to mention that bananas are NOT included. That is annoying...I was so excited to use my banana slicer but found NO BANANAS in the box!

Badly Translated Instructions

So frustrating. I like the idea, but if they're going to ship it with these instructions that were clearly written by someone who doesn't speak English, I might as well not have bothered. I keep throwing the bananas at it as hard as I can, but they just don't make it all the way through. Is it because I'm not strong enough? Is this for men only? Wish I knew what to do.

No more butter knives!

When I think of all the moms out there who let their little children just EAT a banana (Hell-OOOO, choking hazard!), or have them slice it up themselves with a butter knife.... honestly... where is child services?! It's a dangerous world out there, people! When I think banana safety, I think of my good ol' Hutzler 571!

It just sits there like my ex-wife

Leery before buying but luckily my bananas curved to the right. Beware, no instructions! This thing does not work! I tried for hours with $28 worth of bananas and this thing refuses to slice. It just sits there like my ex-wife. I will be returning it just like I did her.

The days of manually cutting banana into pieces are gone ...

The days of manually cutting banana into pieces are gone...I mean let's be honest, ain't nobody got time for that! This little creation completes the task in a little under one second and BAM, perfectly cut pieces ready to be eaten in the most delicate way.

Hint: Practice first

Mine was missing the instruction manual. Had to do a Google search; the only one available was the Hutzler 500 instructions. Was able to tweak the technique, but luckily for me I had a few extra bananas to practice on.

What all the other reviewers fail to tell you is ...

... this comes pre-loaded with Windows Vista. That's right. When I tried to use it the first time, I kept getting a pop-up message telling me to upgrade to Windows 8.1. Not even a mention about a free upgrade to WIndows 10. And it crashed multiple times, while a big pile of bananas on my kitchen counter kept getting browner and browner. I returned it and took my Sawzall back out of the closet.

I was assaulted by a pack of monkeys after using ...

I was assaulted by a pack of monkeys after using this during a camping trip in Belize. I'm still trying to patch back together the shambled pieces I used to call my life. Totally regifting it this Christmas.

Size does matter when it comes to your banana !

I opened the package and immediately was struck with the realization that it's too small, my banana is bigger. Size does matter when it comes to your banana. I guess I will have to wait for the The Hutzler 572 extended size Banana Slicer.

Heads Up: Updated "S " Model Coming Soon

Heads up: rumor has it that a new version of this will be coming out in the fall, rendering all previous models obsolete. That might not be a problem for you, if you have lower standards than I do about staying current. The Hutzler 571S Banana Slicer is rumored to come with a laser level, bluetooth, and facial recognition software. Come September, you can say goodbye to being angry about strangers cutting your bananas.

Go Bananas!!

Best Gluten-Free slicer on the market...

Not made of banana

Don't be fooled by the name, this product is not made out of banana. It doesn't, however, attract fruit flies or turn brown when placed in the refrigerator. So, I guess you pick your battles.

No adapter included

Be warned, this does NOT come with an AC Adapter or USB cable. You're on you're own in that department, amigo.

Instructions unclear.

Banana caught in ceiling fan at first, now stuck in anus.

Perfect hamster stretcher

This slicer has changed my life. I keep one in my first aid kit as a stretcher in case my hamster passes out on a hot summer's day. It's helped me more times than I can count, and I'm adult, so I can really get up there in numbers.

Not needed

I don't need this, I have the app.

Life Changing

For years, my life was a lie. Cut a banana with a knife they said. Just go all Bruce Lee and chop up the banana they said. Well, they were wrong. Only a Hutzler 571 can cut a banana with such precision, such elegance, such sex appeal. On an aside, aliens have been monitoring me, unimpressed. But when I got my hands on this banana slicer, they finally accepted me, since I now have proof of human intelligence and innovation. The aliens as sophisticated as they are, never were able to conceive such a device as this. Thank you Hutzler 575 Banana Slicer, you have single handedly won us favor with extraterrestrial life forms.

The Redeemer

The banana slicer not only saved me time, it saved my soul. I won't bore you with the details as to how.

Great Product, but Estate Planning Headache

Unfortunately some of our 16 kids have been lobbying to be awarded this beloved family heirloom after my wife and I pass on to the great beyond. We have spent tens of thousands of dollars on lawyers writing and re-writing our will in the futile effort to come to some fair arrangement. It looks like we'll end up auctioning this item and evenly splitting the proceeds amongst our heirs.

Yes, we have no bananas

I shoved an entire bunch in this thing at once. It didn't work. Should I remove the outer layers on them first?

No dashboard mount?

I'm only taking off two stars because, to be fair, the description did not include anything about this. That being said, I don't think it was an unreasonable assumption. If they're going to promote this as a productivity tool ("Faster...") then they need to be conscious of their customers' efficiency needs. Unless I can jury-rig a solution, I'm stuck using my passenger seat cutting block.

Banana is. Banana loves. Banana is all.

This banana slicer did not change my life. It did not change the way I see the world. It completed it. Because I see now I was shackled in Plato's cave, blind to the reality of a world that transcends our own. A world where the banana oppressor does not force us to callus our weak hands with banana peels, one where we can escape that cold, forsaken distopia of unsliced bananas. A world where peace has lost all meaning because we are surrounded by it, encompassed by it, engulfed by its banana-y wonder.

...also needs an ethernet port

it is difficult to use when on a rollercoaster.

Update it!

The description says kids love slicing their own bananas but my kids hate this. I think adding a touchscreen display would help.

Dreamcatcher

This is the dreamcatcher I dreamt about. Apart from slicing banners, you can hang it over your bed and get a great night sleep.

Functions Great After You Update Firmware

Functions much better after you update the firmware to 1.4.3 via bluetooth.

Hutzler 571 is the only banana slicer to be deemed worthy by ALL religions!

Finally, no more having to eat bananas in one bite! For years I have been telling people I don't like bananas because it hurts the back of my throat when I eat them! They are just too long! Thanks to the geniuses at Hutzler, who stepped in where evolution could not and allowed us to be able to enjoy the banana pain-free.

Happy with this banana shaped banana slicer.

Does a great job dividing a single banana into multiple pieces. If you've ever had a whole banana and you'd like to cut it into pieces in one fluid motion, this is for you. Help, my father beats me.

Couldn't figure out how to use it

English no so good. Need instructions in Yupik.

Better than my weed whacker

For years now I have been using my weed whacker on my bananas and it works very well, sadly causes my banana to taste like grass. This has saved me time, effort, and money.

Always with me!

Privet, I'm russian. I drink vodka all time. I need snack after shot, to keep going. This thing perfect! 1 pickled cucumber, 18 slices. This good for 18 shots! Na zdorovie, camrads!

It took hutzler 571 models to get it right, but ...

… it does not disappoint. She's a beaut, all right. I only wonder if the rumors of the hutzler 572 are true. Knowing these fat cat corporate giants they'll wait until the end of the year to start rolling them out just in time for the holidays. I hate fat cats!

it works great for threatening the old hubby if you know what ...

What a gadget! I don't just use mine for bananas, it works great for threatening the old hubby if you know what I mean. :)

clever

I don't use this word lightly; I don't use it for any of my kids or members of congress. But this thing slices bananas, so, yeah. Anymore, knives are for cretins, schlemiels, and clods ... which, ironically enough are actually the three monikors I've reserved for my kids.

Best thing since sliced banana!

Best thing since sliced banana!

Great for those lacking opposable thumbs

This banana slicer is a godsend! It is easily manipulated, even if you lack opposable thumbs; there must be a plethora of banana nut bread and banana cream pies and dehydrated banana chips in places like Mississippi and Alabama!

My life is now complete!!!!!!!!!!!!!!!

I work two fulltime jobs (as a wine taster and a rodeo clown), and the last thing I want to do after a long day's work is finger my banana (not to mention, slicing it by hand). Well, now my problem's solved.
Finally....FINALLY, this revolutionary product has hit the shelves!!! The banana gods are smiling down upon us. I would like to thank Mr. Hutzler for inventing this scientific wonder. As far as I'm concerned, he possesses

one of the greatest scientific minds of all time. I would have to rank him right up there with the likes of Leonardo Da Vinci, Albert Einstein, Thomas Edison and that guy who invented the French Tickler.

Here's another problem with it....

Sadly, I have a unique problem. The bananas I bought this week curl neither to the left nor the right; my bananas curl upwards. Nearly sliced my d*** fingers into neat 1" chunks. Guess I'll have to wait for the right-curl bananas to be stocked at my local grocer.

I guess it works?

Who has time to slice their own bananas, what with cat videos on the internet to watch? Not me. So I swallowed this, and now I can swallow my bananas whole. My only problem is that I can't really tell if it is working or not. Well, that, and the vomiting blood. Recommended with reservations.

Five Stars

Hello Hutzler 571, Goodbye Bitter Remorse

Goodbye arthritis...

… Hello time to write that novel I've never talked about.

Five Stars

Finally! I've shaved literal fractions off of my daily routine.

VERY IRRESPONSIBLE packaging.

Bought this for the wife and our (dyslexic) son has sliced ALL of my bandanas. About to get thrown out of my gang. I'm so mad, I could just spit.

A perfect gift for the person who already has everything...

...except for a banana slicer that cuts banana slices thick enough to choke a monkey. Yeah, if they don't have that, then this is a good gift. Assuming of course they want to choke a monkey ... but let's face it, who doesn't? amirite?

Sliced my finger... PERFECTLY!

"Here, catch!" were the last words I recall as the 571 Banana Slicer twirled majestically through the air towards me. I put my hand up to catch it but it sliced my finger... PERFECTLY into 16 pieces. Five stars for the even slicing. Oh, and it's easy to clean too.

This sh*t is bananas.....

Thank you Buddha for this amazing product. I have quickly become known to my townspeople as 'the Woman who slices perfect bananas.' (It's a very well respected skill in my town).

This product also has helped me eat more bananas, shop for bananas every 3 days to keep them in the perfect stages of ripeness and the shape for my tool which in turn gave me purpose in life. I also gained a few pounds with the extra sugar and it seemed to go to my booty , so this product is also a booty enhancer, wow, who knew?

This Hutz is Bananas. B-a-n-a-n-a-s

There was a time in my life when I did not own the Hutzler 571. I will now forever refer to those days as the "dark era". The time saved from having to slice my bananas by hand allows me to focus my time on this things I love to do. Buying bananas for example.

saves my dignity at work!

Guys on the loading doc would line up to pass comments on my technique when I ate my banana for lunch. Now they have to pick on me for something else. So, yeah ... winning!

I had to return it

It was just too complicated for me. There were no clear instructions as to which end of the Hutzler went to which end of the banana. That's okay. I actually hate bananas anyhow.

The rich North have come up with a way to slice up the produce of the poor South.

This tool is clearly an invention of the imperialists. It is a classic example of "divide and rule" in our kitchens – the heart of our homes. It is a conspiracy to taking us apart bit by bit. Is there no justice anywhere?

Save water and time with this environmental leviathan.

The water supply in our area has been inconsistent for the last few years. On most days our shower delivers a lukewarm spattering, the washing machine takes two hours to fill and we can only press full-flush on the toilet if no-one else has been yet that morning. Our household has become a much happier place now we only need a half-flush to say 'cheerio' to the turds. The Hutzler 571 Banana Slicer doubles up wonderfully as a jobby reducer, slicing those loaves into manageable chunks, even for the weakest flush. The enforced waiting time for family toilet visits has reduced significantly, we're thinking about trying Mum without nappies next week.

This may not seem like a big deal until you consider the fact that ...

BE AWARE! The Hutzler 571 is a MANUAL banana slicer, it is NOT automatic. The online product description and the ads in Hutzler Magazine do not tell you this! This may not seem like a big deal until you consider the fact that the Hutzler makes seventeen cuts at once, and therefore requires SEVENTEEN TIMES the amount of force required by a single-cut device like a credit card or whatever else you might currently be using. Now, I'm no 40 pound weakling, but I'm also no Dimitri Martin, and my arms were killing me after I used this thing. This product is NOT for the average consumer with average strength!

I was really stymied to find that perfect gift for our 6th date

I was looking for a gift for a guy here in NYC. I was really stymied to find that perfect gift for our 6th date. Not too extravagant but not cheap. Something appropriate to mark the 6th date milestone. Then I found the Hutzler 571 Banana Slicer. He loved it! Little did I know that before meeting me he had been using banana scissors. Even if it doesn't work out between us (which it probably won't since who uses banana scissors?), I feel I have enriched his life considerably.

Excitement is building here at the lab.

I am at most 2-3 days from successfully reverse-engineering the Hutzler 571 Banana Slicer. I shall post my results and present the DIY plans FREE to the public at a press conference. Yes, hassle-free, banana-slicing is our birthright!

Doesn't work!

Worst banana slicer EVER! I hate peeling bananas. It doesn't make any sense. I mean, I can open a can of peaches, but I have to peel AND cut a banana? Maybe in Sweden, but not here. This is A-freaking-merica!

Anyway, I figured I'd try the thing and it only makes total mush out of the banana and squirts out the end! (try explaining THAT stain!). Just buy the frozen pre-cut bags!

I do not approve of murdering bananas in such an inhumane way.
Put yourself in your banana's shoes and ask yourself this very important question...would I want my banana to do this to me?

Three Stars
Great for bananas. Mediocre for circumcisions.

I lost my wife over this slicer
It's true that this slicer chops bananas into 18 chunks. But Linda was raised by a family who only sliced their bananas into 17 pieces. How was I supposed to know? She left for Duluth the next day to live the life of a rodeo clown now. A sad rodeo clown.

Five Stars
Changed my life ... for about 15 minutes.

Before I discovered the Hutzler 571 Banana Slicer...
...I spent 17 1/2 hours per day looking at inappropriate content on the Internet. Now that I have the Hutzler 571 Banana Slicer, I ... Well, I still look at inappropriate Internet content for 17 1/2 hours out of every day, but my bananas I rely on to replace the potassium in my system are sliced to perfection!

Yeah, sure... If you like "small" bananas.

My bananas are too BIG for this slicer... My banana is all..."hanging" over the edge and "flopping" on the sides. As soon as I get the banana stuffed in...I'm getting complaints of it "hanging out". Gonna need a bigger slicer!

A nonsense verse for Jacques from Grace

big box, small box

pish posh

music, sweet and joyous

rock and roll and blues and funk

pish posh

heartfelt words

watery bits

art and life

pish posh

grace and grit

tender and tough

levity, levity

pish posh

here and now

that day

pish posh

bananas, bananas, bananas

burp

Totally disappointed! I want a refund

It made my butt look big! Totally disappointed! I want a refund!

Rocket science

A lot of people question whether we need the space program. Wouldn't the billions be better spent curing disease or fighting poverty? People who say that don't realize how much better our lives are for the many technological advances that come out of space exploration. As a retired NASA engineer, I see how our work benefits us every day. When people ask me to give an example, I always point to the Hutzler 571 sitting on my counter.

Instructions unclear

Product Description states "Great for Cereal" but instructions unclear. No matter what I do the cereal doesn't end up sliced, it crumbles or large pieces get stuck between sections. I love the banana color and realistic curve. Too bad I don't have any cereal that is soft and banana shaped.

Best thing since sliced bread

Oh. my. GAW YOU CAN SLICE BANANAS?? I've been eating them whole all this time.

Beware of GMOs

I bought this product because of the high reviews not even knowing what it did, but I figured if everyone was rating it so well I had to have one. First, mine didn't come with any directions. After reading reviews and asking questions for 3 days I found out you needed a banana to use it. Naturally my next question was "what the hell is a banana and where do I get one?" Well after 3 more days of asking on my favorite sewing website, I learned you can buy them at food stores, that bananas have nothing to do with sewing machines, and that I'm evidently a jerk for not knowing everything. Long story short, I think this slicer is made of GMOs or something. Now I'm no sciencer, but the banana was a glorious yellow before using the slicer and a few days later it's black and mushy. You can't tell me that's just coincidence! Don't use this product. It's probably not gluten free either.

One Star

Instructions were NOT clear. I set my couch on fire. :(

Get to steppin, delayed cereal toppings

Before I got this product, I had no idea how to slice a banana. I would just stare at it. But it aint goin' down like that anymore, son! I got that new Hutzler joint - boom!

I am giving this product 2 stars instead of 1 ...

I am giving this product 2 stars instead of 1 star only because the emergency room doctor told me he has never seen such perfectly uniform lacerations on one's genitals.

Hutzler finally perfects the banana slicer.

I tried all 570 of Hutzler's previous banana slicers but I can definitely say they've nailed it with the 571. They've finally gotten the shape right after the embarrassing 138, which was really shaped like an apple at best, the 390 which was backwards and, of course, the legendary phallic 560. This is it, the pinnacle of banana slicing technology has finally arrived!

One Star

Banana slicer gave me aids. Gosh darnit.

OOH-OOH-AAH-AAH!!!!!

ooh-oooo-oo-aaaa-ah-aah!! ooooh-oo-ooh!!! ah-oo-oo-ah!! aaaah-ooooooooooo!!!!

Five Stars

Lorena Bobbitt approved this device!

One Star

My wife just bought this. We don't, nor have we ever eaten bananas. I'm just getting a divorce. Seems easier than having a conversation around it.

Thanks, Obama

In my home country, I was a doctor. I was respected. I was somebody. I was stopped in the grocery store, the butcher shop, and the adult video parlor by thankful patients. But times changed and I had to come to America, a place filled with life, liberty, and the promise of beautiful, blonde, buxom women. My unattractive, arranged married wife and kids? Well, sometimes a man has to take care of himself, you know? But, well, the life of a Bangledeshi immigrant in the rolling banana fields of South Dakota isn't quite the FFFFFFM orgy that Fox News would have you believe. So many bananas. So many slices… Still, it was a life, a dream, a chance to be away from that wife. And then one day...it just came to a crashing halt. My master, in his golf cart, drove through those same rolling fields, and told me and the other pickers that we were fired. "The socialist Obama has mandated that we have uniform slicing of bananas. We must use the Hutzler 571 banana slicer. Go back to your home countries and your homely wives!" I'm now writing this review under the highway overpass, sipping out of a bottle that is a combination of whiskey and urine. My clothes are rags I stole off a fellow undomiciled who had died. My life is ruined, my dreams… they are now nightmares. Thanks, Obama Still, I have to give it two stars. The slices are immaculate.

Premature

They released this product too soon. Without the upcoming 513 banana peeler, it's useless.

Size matters with this product.

For years I struggled to cut my bananas into uniform segments. I had given up all hope, and wondered what life was worth living for if my bananas could not be given the proper vivisection they deserved. When I finally saw this product, I felt my prayers had been answered. Imagine my chagrin when the much anticipated product arrived and it turned out my bananas lacked the girth necessary to fit into the slicer. The makers of this product failed to take into account that not all bananas are created equally. I now lose sleep over feelings of inadequacy over the size of my bananas.

One Star

It was pretty good but it was nowhere near as good as Garfield II: A Tale of Two Kitties.

Misleading!!!

I was very disappointed when this product arrived. Calling it a "banana slicer" I naturally assumed it was a slicing machine made out of bananas. You can imagine my outrage when I opened the box and found that it was intended to slice actual bananas. I thought the world was ready for a banana based slicing tool. Obviously I was mistaken.

Don't be lazy

Didn't buy it. I can cut a banana. When did cutting a banana become hard?

Lost mine since it's the EXACT same color of the banana

Painted it blue, and now I can see it, no problem. I'm only giving this 4 stars because it's not offered in other colors.

A new update is coming so wait until it's available ...

A new update is coming so wait until it's available for download to purchase. Fixes minor bugs such as end being cut too close to stem on last slice and loading issues. A new drop down menu will pop up too that will allow user either left hand or right hand settings. New models are coming out with "sun resistant" coating that will keep it from overheating if you leave it in the sun too long. Be sure to get the shock resistant case for even more protection.

Check it off the old Bucket List!

I can now safely remove "Sliced and served the perfect banana slice" off of my bucket list. Thank you Hutzler, I owe you BIG. One comment though...when will you guys come out with a green version so I can slice my not-so-ripe bananas?

Perfect for dehydrating

This is the perfect tool for slicing bananas for dehydrating. By using this tool your banana slices are all the same size and will dehydrate at the same rate.

I left my wife after finding one of these...

...Under her pillow! Men! Protect your BANANA! Next they will feature the double-plum smasher! What has become of Amazon? Horrible.

Backward Bananas

If you live in the southern hemisphere and have bananas that curve the wrong direction, try using this product while looking into a mirror.

German engineering, American excellence.

Like most modern marvels, the Hutzler 571 is a collaboration of the world's greatest minds. Combine the mercilessness of Germany with the appetite of America and you get this masterpiece. It works exactly as promised, like a symphony in the soundtrack of life. My only complaint is that these are probably too affordable. I fear a world in which we eat bananas with such ravenous efficiency that they become extinct, like the majestic dodo bird and the Sony Walkman.

evolve to a higher being!!!

We gave these to the apes at the zoo. They immediately started to evolve. All that extra time not spent on cutting up bananas was used to catch up to the rest of the human race. Too bad Darwin isn't around to see this!

Restoring jobs for America

I'm always concerned about those who encourage illegal immigration of workers who will "do the jobs Americans won't do". I was alarmed when I heard rumors that there was a pool of day laborers offering to slice bananas for the local Nanner Puddin' consortium— for substandard pay and no benefits. With a Chinese made product and American elbow grease, we can stem the influx of those who would erode the American way of life.

ABOUT THE AUTHOR

Señor Mateo El Valiente is an award-winning man, lover, and highly decorated Origami Master (we're talking full contact origami; none of that fold and admire nonsense). He's a humble genius who has graced the pages of The Guinness Book of World Records for speaking in Haiku for 364 straight days; it would have been 365 days, but the judges mistook the word of his final poem, "leave" as a direct command, and obeyed. He can bake 30-minute brownies in 23 minutes flat if he has to, but prefers not to. He is a connoisseur of middle-shelf bourbons. Collector of authentic reproduction Volkswagen print advertisements from the 50's and 60's; when advertising "had real avocados", as Lütz so eloquently puts it. He's affiliated with over 87 secret societies; some of them, like the Sons of Motown, will kill you and all of your descendants just for printing their name. He lives with his much-taller wife, their 3 prodigy children, his perfectly-trained chihuahua, and his wife's rescue dog of unknown decent (Egyptian Foulmouth?), who is the absolute worst. When he's not breeding prize-winning sea monkeys, he can often be found admiring the classiest collection of sandglass art the world has ever known, which he also just so happens to own. He is currently crafting the highly anticipated Part Dos in this series of books, and his somewhat less anticipated fourth child.

Made in the USA
Monee, IL
28 October 2022

16750020R00028